ENDANGERED ANIMALS OF
SOUTH
AMERICA

WORLD
BOOK

a Scott Fetzer company
Chicago
worldbook.com

Staff

Executive Committee

President
Donald D. Keller
Vice President and Editor in Chief
Paul A. Kobasa
Vice President, Sales
Sean Lockwood
Vice President, Finance
Anthony Doyle
Director, Marketing
Nicholas A. Fryer
Director, Human Resources
Bev Ecker

Editorial

Associate Director,
Annuals and Topical Reference
Scott Thomas
Managing Editor,
Annuals and Topical Reference
Barbara A. Mayes
Senior Editor,
Annuals and Topical Reference
Christine Sullivan
Manager, Indexing Services
David Pofelski
Administrative Assistant
Ethel Matthews
Manager, Contracts & Compliance
(Rights & Permissions)
Loranne K. Shields

Editorial Administration

Senior Manager, Publishing
Operations
Timothy Falk

Manufacturing/Production

Director
Carma Fazio
Manufacturing Manager
Sandra Johnson
Production/Technology
Manager
Anne Fritzinger
Proofreader
Nathalie Strassheim

Graphics and Design

Art Director
Tom Evans
Senior Designer
Don Di Sante
Media Researcher
Jeff Heimsath
Manager, Cartographic Services
Wayne K. Pichler
Senior Cartographer
John M. Rejba

Marketing

Marketing Specialists
Alannah Sharry
Annie Suhy
Digital Marketing Specialists
Iris Liu
Nudrat Zoha

Writer

A. J. Smuskiewicz

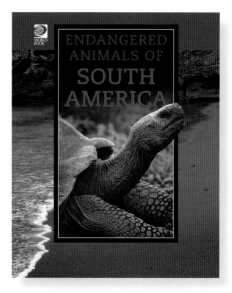

The cover image is the endangered Galapagos giant tortoise.

World Book, Inc.
233 North Michigan Avenue
Chicago, Illinois 60601 U.S.A.

For information about other World Book publications, visit our website at **www.worldbook.com** or call **1-800-WORLDBK (967-5325).**
For information about sales to schools and libraries, call 1-800-975-3250 (United States) or 1-800-837-5365 (Canada).

Library of Congress Cataloging-in-Publication Data

Endangered animals of South America.
    pages cm. -- (Endangered animals of the world)
  Includes index.
  Summary: "Information about some of the more important and interesting endangered animals of South America, including the animal's common name, scientific name, and conservation status; also includes a map showing the range of each animal featured; and a glossary, additional resources, and an index"-- Provided by publisher.
    ISBN 978-0-7166-5626-5
    1. Endangered species--South America--Juvenile literature. I. World Book, Inc
  QL84.3.A1E53 2015
  591.68098--dc23
                                                    2014025609

Endangered Animals of the World
ISBN: 978-0-7166-5620-3 (set)
Printed in China by Shenzhen Donnelley Printing Co., Ltd. Guangdong Province
1st printing October 2014

Contents

Why species in South America are threatened

South America's Amazon rain forest is Earth's largest tropical rain forest and the home of millions of *species* of animals. This rain forest covers approximately 2 million square miles (5.2 million square kilometers) in the basin of the mighty Amazon River. (A species is group of animals or plants that have certain permanent characteristics in common and are able to interbreed.) Most of the Amazon rain forest is located in Brazil, but parts of it lie in eight additional countries. Each year, from 60 to 175 inches (152 to 445 centimeters) of rain fall on the Amazon, and temperatures average about 80 °F (27 °C).

There is a wider variety of wildlife in the Amazon rain forest than in any other natural environment on Earth. The forest contains tens of thousands of plant species. In its natural condition, a typical area of the forest covering 2.5 acres (1 hectare) contains at least 280 species of trees alone. There are as many as 30 million insect species crawling and flying through the forest. More than 1,300 bird species—many of them beautifully colored—live in the Amazon. As many as 3,000 species of fish swim through the forest's rivers and streams. There are also numerous kinds of amphibians, reptiles, mammals, and other animals in the Amazon.

Some 1,700 species in South America are threatened, many critically. Of course, this number includes only those known to science. Many species remain undiscovered. And almost certainly, a number of these animals are in peril or have even disappeared.

Threats. The main threat to South American wildlife is the destruction of the rain forest. Since 1970, in Brazil alone, roughly 300,000 square miles (777,000 square kilometers) of rain forest have been destroyed. This *deforestation* (destruction or damaging of trees) continues today, mainly to make space for ranches for cattle and other livestock; farmland for soybeans, corn, sugar cane, and other crops; plantations for such products as coffee, pineapples, and rubber; gold mines and other mining operations; logging sites for cutting timber; and the construction of roads.

Deforestation is partly the result of South America's expanding human population. Brazil, with approximately 200 million people, is the world's fifth most populous nation. The human population has spread into some of the area originally occupied by rain forest, burning or cutting down the trees in the process. Many *indigenous* (native) people in the Amazon region depend on the forest to support themselves. However, most Amazon deforestation is the result of activities of large corporations, and many of their products are exported to the United States and other wealthy nations.

South America has many other *habitats* (living areas) besides the rain forest. The Andes Mountains, grasslands, dry scrubby forests, deserts, wetlands, and islands are other natural places that are each home to their own kinds of animal communities.

In this volume. The species described in this volume represent the variety of endangered animals in South America. From the smallest and simplest to the largest and most powerful, South America's wildlife is facing challenges from its human neighbors.

Scientific sequence. These species are presented in a standard scientific sequence that generally goes from simple to complex. This sequence starts with insects or other *invertebrates* (animals without backbones) and then moves through fish, amphibians, reptiles, birds, and mammals.

Range. Red areas on maps indicate an animal's *range* (area in which it occurs naturally) on the continent of South America.

Glossary. Italicized words, except for scientific names, appear with their definitions in the Glossary at the end of the book.

Conservation status. Each species discussed in this book is listed with its common name, scientific name, and conservation status. The conservation status tells how seriously a species is threatened. Unless noted differently, the status is according to the International Union for Conservation of Nature (IUCN), a global organization of conservation groups. The most serious IUCN status is *Extinct,* followed by *Extinct in the Wild, Critically Endangered, Endangered, Vulnerable, Near Threatened,* and *Least Concern. Criteria* (rules) used to determine these conservation statuses are included in the list to the right.

Some status designations are according to the United States Fish and Wildlife Service (USFWS), as indicated beneath the species's name.

Conservation statuses

Extinct All individuals of the species have died

Extinct in the Wild The species is no longer observed in its past range

Critically Endangered The species will become extinct unless immediate conservation action is taken

Endangered The species is at high risk of becoming extinct due to a large decrease in range, population, or both

Vulnerable The species is at some risk of becoming extinct due to a moderate decrease in range, population, or both

Near Threatened The species is likely to become threatened in the future

Least Concern The species is common throughout its range

Icons. The icons indicate various threats that have made animals vulnerable to extinction.

Key to icons

 Global warming   Overfishing

 Habitat disturbance   Pet trade

 Habitat loss   Pollution

 Hunting   Ranching

Macrodontia cervicornis

Conservation status: Vulnerable

If you were the size of an insect, you would find this enormous beetle to be extremely frightening. As a person, you might still be frightened by it—or you might think it is an attractive or "cool" creature. It is very big for a beetle—with males growing to an average length of 5 to 5.5 inches (13 to 14 centimeters). Females are a bit smaller. The largest recorded long-horned beetle was about 6.7 inches (17 centimeters) long.

Everything about long-horned beetles seems oversized or unusual. They have long antennae. Their jaws—called mandibles—are long, curved, and sharp and have saw-toothed, or serrated, edges. Their body is black and gold-brown, with a complex pattern of markings on the *elytra* (hard wing coverings). The *larvae* (immature, wormlike forms) of this beetle are even longer than the adults. Some larvae are as long as 8.3 inches (21 centimeters). The larvae are also unusual in not being white, like most beetle larvae. Long-horned beetle larvae are brown, similar to the adults.

Growth. This beetle spends most of its life in its larval form. After hatching from an egg laid under the bark of a dead or dying tree, it may live as a wingless, wormlike larva for 10 years. The larva burrows through the tree, feeding on the rotting wood as it creates spreading, hollow galleries inside the tree. It then turns into an inactive *pupa* (stage in the life of an insect between the larval and the winged adult stages), covered by a hard, protective coat. Inside this coat, the insect develops into a winged adult.

Reproduction. You might think that such a large insect would be too heavy to fly. But the long-horned beetle does fly. As a winged adult, it flies off to find a mate. Females then lay their eggs in trees to start the life cycle all over again. Adults feed on such plant material as leaves, flowers, fruit, and sap. After just a few months as an adult, the beetle dies.

Long-horned beetle

Habitat. Long-horned beetles live in the tropical rain forests of the Amazon Basin—along the Amazon River in South America. Their home range includes the countries of Brazil, Bolivia, Colombia, Ecuador, Guyana, Peru, and Suriname.

Threats. The main danger to the long-horned beetle comes during its long larval stage, when it lives inside trees. At that time, the insect is unable to fly away to escape the downing of the trees. As the rain forest is cleared for logging and to make way for livestock grazing land, and other human developments, the beetle larvae disappear with the lost trees. The missing trees make it hard for surviving adults to find places to lay eggs. Yet another threat to the survival of long-horned beetles is their great demand by insect collectors. These giant beetles are sold for high prices on the international market.

Conservation. Scientists have called for a crackdown on the *poaching* (illegal hunting) of these amazing insects. They also are fighting for greater protection of the beetle's rain forest *habitat* (living area).

The long-horned beetle is big—very big: 5 to 5.5 inches (13 to 14 centimeters) in length. Its size and striking appearance make it popular with collectors, one reason it is endangered.

Zearaja chilensis

Conservation status: Vulnerable

The kite ray is one of more than 500 *species* (types) of fish in the ray family. Some rays, such as this one, are also called skates. Rays are related to sharks, and they resemble sharks in having a boneless skeleton made of *cartilage* (a tough, flexible substance). However, they differ from sharks in having a wide, flat, disklike body with *pectoral fins* (side fins) that look like large wings. They swim gracefully through the sea— usually near the sea floor—by flapping these powerful "wings." Sometimes they just glide through the water without flapping.

Appearance. The body of the kite ray is mostly grayish with some white and reddish blotches. And it really is shaped much like a kite. Its shape is called a rhomboid, a twisted plane figure with two parallel sides of equal length, and two other of a different, but also equal, length. This ray's body is at least 5.6 feet (1.7 meters) wide, with a pointed snout and a long tail. There are numerous spiky "thorns" on top of the body. These thorns are a type of armor that helps the fish defend itself against enemies. The eyes are on top of the body, and the mouth (with many sharp teeth), nostrils, and gill slits are on the bottom.

Habitat. Kite rays, like most other rays, live on and near the sea floor. This species lives along the soft sandy and muddy depths of South America's *continental shelf* (sea floor that slopes from the shore to about 330 feet [100 meters] deep) in the southwestern Atlantic and southeastern Pacific Oceans. Kite rays are found in the Atlantic from southern Brazil to southern Argentina, and in the Pacific off the coast of Chile. They eat fish, clams, oysters, and *crustaceans* (hard-shelled animals) that they find at the bottom of the sea.

Biologists believe that rays are intelligent fish. They base this belief on the fact that rays have a large brain, compared with the size of

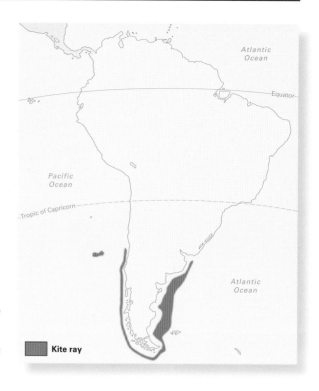

Kite ray

the rest of their bodies. This belief is also based on observations that rays are curious about their surroundings. Many human divers have reported being approached by rays in the water, as if the fish are wondering what the people are doing.

Threats. Kite rays are threatened by the combination of *commercial* (business) catches by the fishing industry and traditional fishing by local people. The rays are caught on purpose for food, and they are also caught accidentally by people seeking other fish or shellfish. The "wings" of the rays are valued because they have a sweet taste. The wing meat is often sold as "imitation scallop." As a result of this overfishing, the kite ray has become *overexploited* (killed to the point that its population has becomes greatly reduced and threatened).

Conservation actions for kite rays include studying their populations and limiting how many can be caught. The governments of Chile and Argentina have laws to manage kite ray populations, but these laws are often ignored.

The kite ray gets its name from its kitelike shape. Like sharks, rays have a boneless skeleton made of cartilage.

Hippocampus ingens

Conservation status: Vulnerable

The Pacific seahorse is a giant among sea-horses, measuring more than 1 foot (30 centimeters) in length. It has the typical seahorse shape—including a head that looks like that of a tiny horse. The head has a long snout and is covered with hard, bony plates, as is the rest of the body. The tail is long, flexible, and strong, which comes in handy when the seahorse wants to hold onto underwater objects. Individuals of this *species* (type) may be any of several colors, including shades of brown, gray, green, red, or yellow. Their color changes to match their surroundings. This type of *camouflage* (disguise) helps the fish hide from enemies.

Habitat. The surroundings of the Pacific seahorse typically include colorful coral reefs. The seahorses prefer branching, treelike corals called gorgonions, to which they can cling with their tails. They also cling to kelp, which is a type of large brown *algae* (seaweed) that grows near the ocean surface in floating "forests." The coral reefs and kelp forests inhabited by the Pacific seahorse are in shallow water ranging from San Diego Bay to the coast of Peru.

As the Pacific seahorse swims through its marine *habitat* (living area), it moves its large *dorsal fin* (back fin) back and forth as much as 35 times a second. This speedy fin action propels the seahorse forward.

Diet. Pacific seahorses are usually active at night, when they hunt for such small animals as mysid shrimp and other *crustaceans* (hard-shelled animals). When a Pacific seahorse finds an animal to its liking, it sucks the prey into the tubelike mouth at the end of its snout. Pacific seahorses are often eaten by tuna and other large fish.

Reproduction. The Pacific seahorse reproduces in the special way that is unique to seahorses—the male carries the young in his

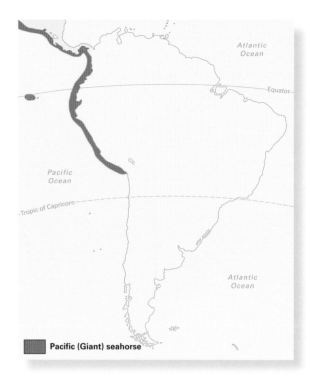

Pacific (Giant) seahorse

body. After mating, the female lays dozens of eggs inside a pouch under the male's tail.

Threat. The Pacific seahorse population is declining. People catch and dry the seahorses to sell on the international market. The dead seahorses are used in Asia and elsewhere to make traditional medicines. Many tons of Pacific seahorse are caught and shipped to Asia every year for this purpose. Living and dead seahorses are also sold to collectors for display. Many seahorses are killed accidentally in a fishing practice called trawling, in which a ship drags a huge funnel-shaped net through the sea to catch shrimp or other shellfish or fish.

Yet another threat to the seahorses is damage to their coastal habitats. Part of this problem is caused by the construction of buildings, roads, and other developments near the Mexican, Central American, and South American coasts for tourism, housing, and other purposes. The developments lead to water pollution, increased *sediment* (soil and other matter that flows into water), or changes in the *salinity* (salt level) of the water.

The beautiful Pacific seahorse is 1 foot (30 centimeters) in length, one of the largest of the known species of seahorses.

Phyllobates terribilis

Conservation status: Endangered

Golden poison frogs are small, brightly colored amphibians found in the hilly rain forests along the coast of the Pacific Ocean in Colombia. The colors of the frogs vary depending on their exact locations. Some are golden yellow, golden orange, or deep orange. Others are pale green or greenish yellow. All these frogs have big black eyes, and most have black edging around the *tympanum* (the round outer membrane that sends sound waves to the frog's inner ear).

In nature, bright colors are often warnings that an animal is poisonous. The bright colors are like a sign telling predators, "You'd better leave me alone or you'll be sorry!" Such is the case with golden poison frogs. Their skin contains large amounts of *toxic* (poisonous) chemical compounds. These compounds—with the tongue-twisting names of batrachotoxin and homobatrachotoxin—can cause deadly nerve and heart problems in people who get even small doses of the chemicals inside their bodies. The skin of a single frog, which is less than 2 inches (5 centimeters) long, contains enough poison to kill 10 people—or 22,000 mice. Golden poison frogs are the most toxic frogs known.

Species. This species is one of three *species* (types) of frog used by tribal people in Colombia to obtain poison for their blow-gun darts. The people first capture the frogs live. Then they carefully rub the darts over the skin of the frogs to smear the poison on the darts. Finally, they shoot the poisoned darts with their blow guns—tubes that they blow into—to hunt and kill other animals.

Few predators attack golden poison frogs—except for the fire-bellied snake, which can eat the frogs without dying or becoming ill because its body has a natural *immunity* (resistance) to the frog's poison. The snake has a substance in its body that makes the poison harmless.

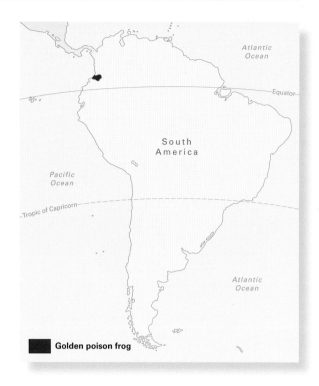

Golden poison frog

Habitat and diet. Golden frogs live in the western foothills of the Andes Mountains. They usually stay on the forest floor, where they eat insects, spiders, worms, and other small *invertebrates* (animals without backbones).

Threat. As the rain forest continues to be cut and burned down, the population of golden poison frogs is becoming smaller and smaller. Parts of the forest are being destroyed by logging. Other parts are being cleared for crops or grazing land for livestock. Chemical pesticides, fertilizers, and other pollutants have contaminated the land and water. These are all threats to the frogs. Yet another problem is the illegal collection of the frogs for the pet market.

Conservation. One reason it is important to protect golden poison frogs is that they are valuable members of the rain forest ecosystem. But another reason to save this species—and other species of poison frogs—is that scientists could learn how to make useful medicines from studying the frogs' toxins. For example, batrachotoxin could be made into a drug that helps reduce pain.

The skin of the golden poison frog contains toxic chemical compounds, which the tribal people of the region use to coat their poison-laced darts.

Oophaga lehmanni

Conservation status: Critically Endangered

The red-banded *species* (type) of poison frog—which is even more endangered than the golden poison frog (pp. 12-13)—is known by a number of common names. "Red-banded" and *"harlequin"* refer to the bright red, orange, or yellow bands that mark the frog's otherwise black or brown body. (A harlequin is a type of clown who wears multicolored tights.) Another name—Lehmann's frog—honors Federico Carlos Lehmann Valencia (1914-1974), a Colombian biologist and conservationist. Lehmann traveled throughout Colombia studying wildlife and collecting specimens for universities and the government.

The color pattern on these tiny frogs varies from one individual to another, like fingerprints. As with the golden poison frog, the bright, bold colors serve as a warning to predators that eating the frog will sicken or kill them. Red-banded poison frogs grow no longer than 1.4 inches (3.6 centimeters).

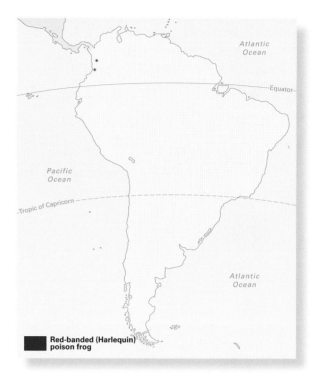

Red-banded (Harlequin) poison frog

Habitat and diet. Red-banded poison frogs can be found hopping across the ground and sitting on leaves in the tropical rain forest of Colombia. The species is known to exist in only a few places in the forest. The frogs hunt on the forest floor during the daytime. Their diet consists of such small *invertebrates* (animals without backbones) as insects, spiders, and worms.

Reproduction. Males attract females by making special calls consisting of a series of notes. When a female is attracted to a particular male, she lays a bunch of sticky eggs on leaves above the ground in the male's territory. The male then fertilizes the eggs with his sperm. He also cares for the eggs by guarding them and changing their positions every now and then so that all the eggs get enough oxygen. After two to four weeks, he carries the eggs on his back to new areas, putting each egg in a different spot—such as water-filled places in bromeliad plants or bamboo stalks. He does this so that the tadpoles cannot eat each other after they hatch from the eggs. The female feeds the tadpoles unfertilized eggs, which she deposits in water near them. The tadpoles turn into adult frogs over a period of two or three months.

Threat. The main reasons that red-banded poison frog became critically endangered were the destruction of its rain forest *habitats* (living areas) and its capture for the pet market. The trees of the forest were cut down for timber and burned down to create space for grazing land and crops. The remaining slices of rain forest in the region are isolated from each other—a problem called habitat *fragmentation*. This is a problem for frogs and other types of animals, because it makes it almost impossible for their populations to grow and spread.

When red-banded poison frogs had a larger population, they were frequently captured for sale as pets around the world. Unfortunately, many of those frogs died during the handling or shipping processes. Today, the frogs are so rare that almost none of them are collected for pets.

The red-banded poison frog is endangered by loss of habitat and by its one-time popularity in the pet trade.

Rhinoderma darwinii

Conservation status: Vulnerable

This small frog was discovered by, and named after, Charles Darwin, the British naturalist who developed the theory of *evolution by natural selection* in the 1800's. According to that theory, all *species* (types) of living things developed gradually from a common ancestor over many millions of years by a branching process.

The Darwin's frog grows to a maximum length of only about 1.2 inches (3 centimeters). The head has a strange triangular shape. It looks that way because this frog has a long, pointed *proboscis* (snout). The frog's coloring ranges from bright green to brown to some combination of green and brown. The colors of the upper body help the frog hide among the leaf litter on the forest floor. The lower parts of the frog are black and white.

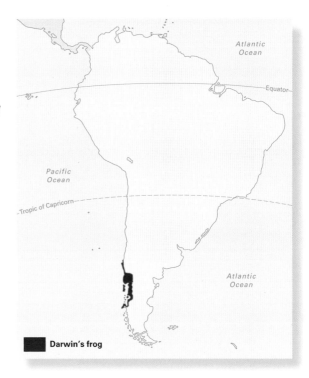

Darwin's frog

Habitat. Darwin's frog lives in the cool forests of central and southern Chile and Argentina. Unlike temperatures in the better known Amazonian rain forest, the temperature in these forests normally stays between 41 °F and 70 °F (5 °C and 21 °C). Darwin's frogs are usually found along stream banks in the forests. They hunt for insects, worms, and other tiny animals during the day.

Reproduction. Male frogs court females by making ringing, bell-like calls. The female lays about 40 eggs on the ground. The male guards the eggs while the tadpoles grow inside. When the tadpoles are almost ready to hatch—in approximately 20 days—the male licks up the eggs with his tongue and puts them into a pouch under his throat and stomach. The pouch is called a vocal sac. This is an unusual use for a frog's vocal sac. The males of most other species of frogs use their vocal sacs only to make loud calls.

After the eggs are inside the male's vocal sac, they hatch into tadpoles. The tadpoles live in the vocal sac for several days as they go through the stages of *metamorphosis*—gradually changing from fishlike tadpoles with tails to little frogs with legs. When metamorphosis is almost complete, the male spits out the froglets.

Darwin's frogs display an interesting behavior when they are frightened by a predator or other threat. They roll over onto their backs, stop moving, and pretend that they're dead. Sometimes they do this after they jump into a stream, where they float upside down on the water's surface. The predator loses interest in the "dead" frog.

Threats. It is not so easy for the frogs to escape the destruction of their forest *habitat*s (living areas). Many of their habitats have been destroyed by *clearcutting* (the removal of all trees in an area). After people cut down the native trees, they often plant pine or eucalyptus trees, which can be made into useful products. The frogs cannot survive when their habitat is changed so drastically. The native forest habitat has also been reduced because of droughts.

In some areas, populations of Darwin's frogs have disappeared for reasons that scientists do not understand.

The male Darwin's frog with a froglet that he has just spit out from his vocal sac. The tadpoles live in the father's vocal sac as they morph into little frogs with legs.

Conolophus subcristatus
Conservation status: Vulnerable

The Galapagos land iguana is a large lizard that lives on six of the Galapagos Islands, a group of many islands in the Pacific Ocean west of Ecuador. Observations of the unusual animal life on these islands by British naturalist Charles Darwin in 1835 formed the basis of his theory of *evolution by natural selection* (the theory that all *species* [types] of living things developed gradually from a common ancestor over many millions of years by a branching process.)

The Galapagos land iguana can grow to a length of 3.3 feet (1 meter) and a weight of 28.7 pounds (13 kilograms). This big lizard looks like it might have survived from the Age of the Dinosaurs. Its rough, scaly body is mostly yellowish, marked with patches of brown, black, and white. Down the middle of its back is a ridge of sharp spines. Its feet are large, wide, and strong, with long, sharp claws.

Galapagos land iguana

Habitat and diet. The land iguanas use their powerful feet to dig burrows into the hard, dry ground, where they sleep at night. During the day, the reptiles forage for food over the rocky landscape of the Galapagos. They eat mainly plants, especially the thick, fleshy parts of cactus plants. Sometimes they tear out the cactus spines with their claws before eating the plants. The water inside the cactuses is a major source of drinking water for the iguanas in their dry *habitat* (living area).

On warm sunny mornings, land iguanas like to bask in the sun while lying on rocks. But when it gets too hot in the middle of the day, they'll hide in the shade of rocks or plants. That is how these reptiles keep a stable body temperature.

Mutualism. The land iguanas keep themselves free of pesky ticks with the help of finches, of which there are several species on the islands. The little birds pick the ticks off the iguanas and eat the blood-sucking pests. The iguanas will often shift their bodies to make it easier for the finches to get at the ticks, such as by raising their bellies off the ground. This relationship between the reptiles and birds is a type of *mutualism* (any relationship between two different species in which both benefit).

Threat. The land iguana population has shrunk because of the growing human population on the Galapagos Islands. A variety of human activities—including construction, tourism, and the introduction of *alien* (nonnative) species—have harmed the land iguanas and their habitat. Introduced cats, dogs, and rats eat young iguanas and iguana eggs. Introduced goats destroy the plants that iguanas eat. The natural plant life of the islands has also been harmed by such introduced plants as elephant grass, which has spread over and changed natural areas.

Conservation. Conservationists are working to save land iguanas in two main ways. They are breeding iguanas in the safe conditions of captivity and then releasing the offspring into the wild. And they are trying to remove the alien predators and plants from the islands.

The Galapagos Island iguana has become vulnerable because of the introduction into its habitat of alien species, for example, cats, dogs, and rats.

Amblyrhynchus cristatus
Conservation status: Vulnerable

The Galapagos marine iguana is the ocean version of the Galapagos land iguana. It is the only *species* (type) of lizard that spends much time in the sea. Marine iguanas live on the coastal rocks of the Galapagos Islands, where they usually eat ocean *algae* (seaweed) that they can scrape off the rocks when the tide is low. But when the tide is high, they may have to dive underwater—as deep as 80 feet (25 meters)— to get to the algae. Only the largest, heaviest individuals are able to do that.

When food is hard to find, the bones and bodies of marine iguanas become smaller. The smaller size means that the lizards need less energy and can survive on less food.

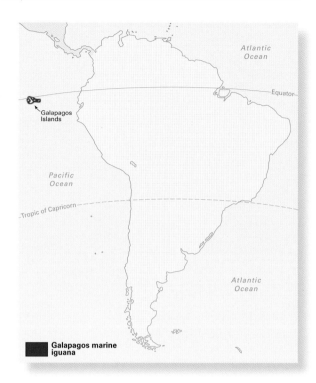

Galapagos marine iguana

Appearance. Marine iguanas are smaller than land iguanas. Males, which are larger than females, grow to an average length of 2.5 feet (0.75 meter). Marine iguanas are mostly gray or black. However, parts of their bodies may turn greenish or reddish during the summertime breeding season. Biologists believe that this color change may be the result of eating a certain species of algae that is most common at that time of year.

Habitat. Marine iguanas cannot stay in seawater for long periods because ocean currents cause the water around the Galapagos Islands to be very cold. If reptiles are exposed to low temperatures for too long, they will die. So the marine iguanas have to crawl out of the cold sea and onto the land, where they try to find a warm, dry spot in the sun.

To warm up, the reptiles often lay on top of rocky cliffs. But during the hottest times of day, the iguanas hide in the shade under rocks or other cool places. "Cold-blooded" reptiles have to move around to keep their body temperature steady. That makes them different from "warm-blooded" mammals—like people—that have bodies that can maintain a steady internal temperature, even when their environment is very hot or cold.

Reproduction. Female marine iguanas scratch out nests for their eggs in sand or volcanic ash on land. In the deep pit she digs into the ground, she lays from one to six eggs. She watches over the nest for about three months— guarding the eggs against predators—until the eggs hatch. As soon as the young iguanas break out of their shells, they are on their own.

Threats. Galapagos marine iguanas face some of the same threats that challenge their land-based cousins. For example, cats, dogs, and rats that were brought by people to the Galapagos Islands eat young marine iguanas and iguana eggs. Other threats to the marine reptiles are different. Marine iguana populations are harmed by oil spills and other forms of ocean pollution. The marine populations can also be affected by *El Niño* (a natural change in Pacific Ocean currents that recurs every several years). In some years, these changes cause declines in the algae species eaten by the iguanas.

The Galapagos marine iguana is the only species of lizard that spends time in the sea. Because of cold temperatures they are exposed to in the ocean, marine iguanas need to sun themselves on land to raise their body temperature.

Chelonoidis nigra

Conservation status: Endangered

Yet another large, threatened reptile of the Galapagos Islands, the Galapagos giant tortoise can grow to a length of about 4 feet (1.2 meters) and a weight of more than 660 pounds (300 kilograms). It is the largest tortoise living today.

The *carapace* (top shell) of this tortoise has different shapes, depending on the particular island where the animals live. Those that live on the larger, wetter islands tend to have dome-shaped shells. Those that live on smaller, drier islands tend to have saddle-shaped shells, as well as longer legs and necks. Biologists explain these differences by noting that many of the plants that tortoises eat on the dry islands are tall. The front of the saddle-shaped shell of those tortoises is bent upward, making it easier for the reptiles to raise their head to reach the high parts of the plants that they like.

Diet. Galapagos giant tortoises eat cactus fruits, various flowers, and grasses. They graze during the warmest times of the day. They often wallow in small pools that form during heavy rains. Like the Galapagos land iguana, the giant tortoise benefits from finches that pick off ticks.

Reproduction. During mating season, male giant tortoises compete with each other to stake out territory. When two males approach each other, they both try to appear bigger by standing up taller and stretching out their necks. The females dig nests into the ground, where they lay their eggs. They keep them warm by burying them beneath soil and plant matter.

Lifespan. Galapagos giant tortoises can live for more than 150 years. One female, named Harriet, is thought to have been 176 years old when she died in a zoo in Australia in 2006. According to historical records, British naturalist Charles Darwin collected Harriet when he visited the Galapagos Islands in the 1830's.

Galapagos giant
tortoise

Threats. There were so many giant tortoises on the Galapagos Islands when Spanish *mariners* (sailors) first arrived there in the 1600's that the mariners named the islands after the tortoises. *Galapagos* means *tortoise* in Spanish. But the tortoise population soon began to decline. The Spanish mariners and later sealers, whalers, and pirates captured the big reptiles for food. The tortoises were also killed to get the oil from the fatty parts of their skin. People used this oil for lamps, varnishes, cosmetics, and medicines.

Other threats to the Galapagos giant tortoise have come from dogs, cats, and rats that people brought to the islands. These predators can easily kill the young tortoises before their carapace has completely formed.

All these threats caused giant tortoise numbers to plummet from more than 250,000 in the 1600's to only about 3,000 by the 1970's. At that time, scientists began raising young tortoises in captivity until they are strong enough to protect themselves. The captive-bred tortoises are released in Galapagos National Park.

Galapagos giant tortoises were once so numerous that Spanish sailors named their island habitat *Galapagos*, the Spanish word for *tortoise*. They were hunted for both food and body oil, but it was the introduction of such nonnative species as cats, dogs, and rats that decimated their population.

Podocnemis expansa

Conservation status: Near Threatened

This turtle is known by many names—including tartaruga, arrau, South American river turtle, and giant South American turtle. *Tartaruga* is the Portuguese word for *turtle*. Whatever its name, the tartaruga is the largest river turtle in South America. It grows to an average length of 42 inches (107 centimeters) and a weight of 198 pounds (90 kilograms). Its olive-green *carapace* (top shell) is wide, smooth, and flattish. This shape helps the turtle swim quickly because water flows easily over the shell.

Diet. The turtle has a long, flexible neck that helps it reach plant and *algae* (seaweed) food in the water, including leaves and other plant parts that fall onto the water surface. It also sometimes eats small aquatic *invertebrates* (animals without backbones) that it captures.

Habitat. The tartaruga lives mainly in branches of the Amazon River that have sandy banks and *sand bars* (ridges of sand formed by the action of tides or currents). Its *range* (area in which it is normally found) covers an area from northern Brazil to northern Peru. The turtles also live on Trinidad and Tobago, two islands in the Caribbean Sea near the northeast coast of South America.

Reproduction. Groups of female tartarugas lay as many as 125 leathery eggs in a clutch in the same sandy riverbanks and sand bars every year. In roughly 45 days, the eggs hatch. Female hatchlings tend to come from eggs that are incubated at higher temperatures, and males tend to come from eggs that are incubated at lower temperatures. This relationship between hatchling sex and egg incubation temperature is also true for many other *species* (types) of turtles.

Threats. The population of tartarugas has been reduced by a number of threats. Among these threats are *poaching* (illegal killing) for the

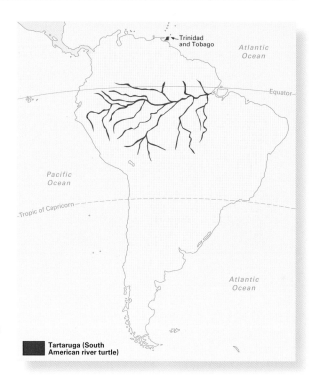

Tartaruga (South American river turtle)

turtles' meat and oil (taken from their fat); the collection of eggs and hatchlings; and the building of industrial sites, cities, and roads near nesting areas. Cutting of forests near the turtles' river *habitat*s (living areas) and damming of the rivers sometimes cause the flooding of nesting sites. The floods may destroy the eggs.

Conservation actions have greatly helped the tartaruga. But, according to the IUCN, continued conservation measures are needed to protect the species. Such measures include limiting the effects of human populations on river habitats and making sure that strong conservation programs are in place.

In one such conservation program—at the Middle Orinoco River in Venezuela—strict rules protect nesting sites, and hatchlings are cared for in captivity until they can be safely released into the wild. This program also includes environmental education for the public, to help people better understand the value of protecting tartarugas and their habitats.

The tartaruga, or the South American river turtle, grows to an average length of 42 inches (107 centimeters) and can weigh as much as 198 pounds (90 kilograms). Their numbers have been reduced by poaching and loss of habitat.

Vultur gryphus

Conservation status: Endangered (USFWS)

A giant among flying birds, the Andean condor is a type of vulture with a wingspread of about 10 feet (3 meters). Its body is as long as 4.3 feet (1.3 meters), and it weighs up to 30 pounds (15 kilograms). This is larger than the more seriously endangered California condor.

Habitat. Andean condors live in the Andes Mountains and along the coasts of Peru and Argentina. They may be found high in the mountains, low in grasslands and deserts, and near the sea. Their bodies are mostly covered in black and white feathers. Around the base of the neck is a collar of white feathers. The featherless neck and head are yellow to dark gray. Males have a fleshy crest on the head and wattles on the neck. Those traits make the Andean condor the only American vulture in which males and females show obvious physical differences—a characteristic known as sexual dimorphism.

Andean condors are powerful, graceful fliers. They can soar and glide for long distances while flapping their wings only once every hour. They don't need to flap often because their long, wide wings ride on top of thermal updrafts, currents of warm air that rise off the ground.

Diet. As the condors fly, they use their keen eyesight to search the ground for food. They can identify food from several miles (kilometers) away. Like other vultures, condors eat mostly *carrion* (the remains of dead animals). Their prey may include the bodies of cattle, llamas, sheep, seals, and sea birds. Their large feet and sharp claws grip the carrion, while they use their sharp, hooked beaks to rip off chunks of meat.

Reproduction. Condors mate for life. The male wins his mate by performing a courtship display in which he spreads his wings and makes loud clicking noises with his tongue. The female lays one or two eggs on bare

Andean condor

ground inside a cave, in a hole, or among boulders. The male and female take turns incubating the eggs and caring for the hatchlings. A young condor needs a lot of care. It cannot fly until it is six months old, and it may need help finding food for two years. Because of all the effort needed to raise a chick, a female Andean condor can reproduce only every other year.

Threats. The condors' slow reproduction rate is one reason that the threats to the birds are serious. Ranchers and farmers kill the vultures out of fear that the big birds will attack their livestock—even though condors hardly ever kill live animals. The condors also die after they eat poisoned bait put out to kill mountain lions and foxes. Because the condors mate for life, the death of either the male or female will leave the surviving member of the pair caring for a chick all by itself. This is a difficult task for a single parent, and the chick may end up dying.

Conservation. Captive-breeding programs are helping to rebuild the population of Andean condors.

The Andean condor, with its 10-foot-
(3-meter-) long wingspread, can glide
for long periods along thermal updrafts.
It can spot food, nearly always carrion,
from miles away.

Approximately 18 *species* (types) of large, colorful, long-tailed parrots known as macaws live in the forests of South America, Central America, and Mexico. They are the largest parrots in the world, with some reaching a length of 3.3 feet (1 meter). Many macaw species are endangered.

Blue-throated macaw

Ara glaucogularis

Conservation status: Critically Endangered (IUCN) Endangered (USFWS)

The blue-throated macaw survives in only one small area of Bolivia. Fewer than 500 individuals may remain in the wild.

Conservationists have tried to protect the bird, but the population continues to decrease. These birds have trouble finding nesting sites in trees as forests have shrunk due to human activities, making them vulnerable to competition from other large birds as well as bats.

Blue-throated macaw

Great green macaw

The blue-throated macaw (right) now exists only in one small area of Bolivia. Scientists fear that as few as 1,000 to 3,000 individual great green macaws (below) survive in the wild.

Great green macaw
Ara ambiguous

Conservation status: Proposed Endangered (USFWS)

The great green macaw survives in small populations in Costa Rica, Colombia, Ecuador, Honduras, Nicaragua, and Panama. Scientists have incomplete data on this species. But the data they have suggest that the population is between 1,000 and 3,000 individuals.

Threats. As with many other species of macaw, destruction of the bird's *habitat* (living area) and the pet trade are the most serious threats to the great green macaw. The macaw's forests are cut down to harvest timber, to build roads and cities, and to clear land for planting bananas, cocoa, and oil palms and for raising cattle and other livestock.

The worst part of habitat destruction for this species is the loss of the almendro tree (also called the mountain almond tree). The great green macaw depends on this tree for both nesting sites and food (the fruit), but the tree is getting harder to find in the shrinking forests.

These beautiful birds have also long been caught and sold as caged pets. Like other parrots, macaws are intelligent and can learn to "talk" (that is, to mimic the sound of words).

However, many people who get macaws for pets soon feel sorry that they did. The birds scream a lot; they bite; they throw up their food; and—if let out of their cages—they tear up woodwork and other items in the home with their large, strong beaks.

Conservation. Classifying any animal species as endangered involves the careful review of scientific data on the population of the species as well as the threats to the species. The IUCN and the USFWS use different *criteria* (rules) when making these classifications.

In 2012 and 2013, researchers with the United States Fish and Wildlife Service (USFWS) announced that several species of macaw deserved classification and protection as endangered species. These included the blue-throated, great green, hyacinth, military, and scarlet macaws. Such classification allows the United States government to regulate imports, exports, and certain other activities that might harm the species.

Such classifications also open the door for other scientists to share their views on the conservation status of a species. In 2013, the USFWS officially classified the blue-throated macaw as endangered. As of 2014, the USFWS was still considering the status of the hyacinth, military, and scarlet macaws.

Spheniscus mendiculus

Conservation status: Endangered

How can penguins—most of which live in Antarctica, the coldest part of the world—live in the center of the tropics? The Galapagos penguin lives on the Galapagos Islands, right on the *equator* (the imaginary line that divides the Northern and Southern hemispheres). Most of the penguins live on the western islands of Isabela and Fernandina, but some live on islands farther east in the Galapagos group.

The Galapagos penguin has several special behavioral *adaptations* that help it live in such a warm *habitat* (living area). (Adaptations are traits that makes an organism better able to survive and reproduce in its environment). One behavior is spending the hottest daytime hours in the sea, where they look for small fish to eat. As anyone who enjoys swimming in the summer knows, it's easier to stay cool in water than on land.

When on land, the penguins cool off by standing with their wings spread out, allowing their body heat to escape from the wings. They also hunch their body forward, so that their bare feet are shaded. Body heat escapes better from skin in the shade than from skin exposed to the sun. That is also why the birds stay in shaded spots as much as possible. When in the sun, the penguins pant to let body heat escape through their mouth. That behavior is similar to the way dogs pant on hot days.

Reproduction and diet. Unlike most other penguins, which breed once a year, the Galapagos penguin may breed as many as three times every year. However, that happens only in years when a steady supply of their food (fish) can be found.

The fish supply becomes reduced during periods known as El Niño Southern Oscillations (ENSO's), when the Pacific Ocean's surface waters warm up and the nutrients in the waters decline. ENSO's occur in the time between the two events known as El Niño and La Niña,

Galapagos penguin

which are complex interactions between Earth's atmosphere and the tropical waters of the Pacific. El Niño and La Niña events occur every two to seven years. During ENSO's, penguins stop breeding until their food supply increases.

Threats. There are fewer Galapagos penguins than any other kind of penguin. Biologists estimate that the population size is about 1,000. The population was greatly reduced by severe ENSO events in the 1980's and 1990's. Many scientists believe that ENSO events are becoming more drastic as a result of long-term climate change caused mainly by human activities, especially the burning of *fossil fuels* (coal, natural gas, and crude oil).

Galapagos penguins have also been harmed in other ways. Many penguins have been killed by cats that were brought to the Galapagos Islands by people. Mosquitoes, which arrived on the islands in the 1980's because of human activities, have spread a disease called *avian* (bird) malaria among the penguins. Some penguins have been accidentally killed when they got caught in floating fishing nets.

The Galapagos penguin is the world's rarest penguin species. It is also the only penguin that lives in the tropics.

Priodontes maximus

Conservation status: Vulnerable

Armadillos are prehistoric-looking mammals with bony plates on their upper body. There are several *species* (types) of armadillos, each with its own type of bony *carapace* (top shell). The giant armadillo has a brown carapace made of from 11 to 13 plates of armor that are fitted and hinged closely together across the animal's back. More plates cover the animal's neck. This carapace provides the armadillo with protection against predators and other enemies. However, rather than hiding in its shell, the armadillo is more likely to run into its burrow or quickly dig itself a hole to hide in at the first sign of danger.

Appearance. The giant armadillo's body reaches a length of about 5 feet (1.5 meters). Its tail adds another several inches to its length. Giant armadillos may weigh more than 100 pounds (50 kilograms). This animal is much larger than the more common nine-banded armadillo, which ranges from the southern United States to Uruguay. That armadillo grows to a length of only about 2 feet (61 centimeters).

Habitat. The giant armadillo lives in grasslands and rain forests in South America, mostly within the vast basin of the Amazon River. Although it is found across a wide section of the Amazon Basin, people rarely see the big animals. That is because the armadillos are thinly scattered throughout their *range* and active mainly at night. (Range is the area in which a species normally lives.) In addition, giant armadillos sometimes do not leave their burrows for days. Their elusive behaviors have made it difficult for scientists to learn much about them.

Diet. These animals have long, strong claws for digging burrows and searching for their food, which consists mostly of insects. Giant armadillos rip open ant and termite mounds with their front claws. Their third claw—which is shaped

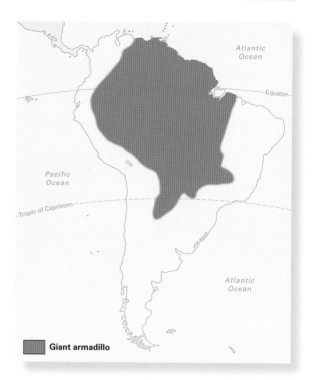

Giant armadillo

like a sharp, curved tool called a sickle—is especially useful for slashing away at the mounds. The armadillos lap up the insects with their sticky tongue. Giant armadillos sometime also eat spiders, worms, snails, and even fruit. They have more teeth than almost any other mammal—from 80 to 100.

Reproduction. Female giant armadillos give birth to one or two young. The young stay inside the burrow with the mother until they are able to catch and eat insects on their own.

Threats. The huge size and great strength of giant armadillos cannot protect them against the threats they face from humans. Many local people hunt them for meat. They are the main source of protein for some people. Many local farmers kill the armadillos out of fear that the big animals will trample on and destroy their crops. Adding to these problems is the clearing of the armadillo's rain forest *habitat* (living area) to make way for farmland and other human developments.

People capture giant armadillos alive and sell them illegally to animal collectors for large amounts of money. While the criminal makes a lot of cash, the armadillos usually die in captivity.

The giant armadillo is native to grasslands and rain forests of South America, primarily in the vast Amazon Basin. It is threatened by hunting and habitat loss.

Short-tailed chinchilla
Chinchilla brevicaudata
(or C. chinchilla)
Conservation status: Critically Endangered

Long-tailed chinchilla
Chinchilla lanigera
Conservation status: Critically Endangered

Chinchillas are small rodents famous for their soft, thick, shiny fur. People have long used chinchilla pelts to make expensive, luxurious coats. It may take pelts from 150 chincillas to make one full-length coat. These attractive animals have also been collected as pets. The hunting of chinchillas in the past led to drastic declines in their populations.

The chunky bodies of chinchillas measure from 11 to 18 inches (28 to 46 centimeters) in length, including a bushy tail. Females are larger than males. Their much-admired blue-gray fur is 1 inch (2.5 centimeters) or more in length. The reason the fur feels so soft and thick is because about 60 hairs grow out of each hair follicle.

Species and habitat. The two *species* (types) of chinchillas—the short-tailed and long-tailed chinchilla—look almost identical. The short-

Short-tailed
chinchilla

Long-tailed
chinchilla

tailed version has a thicker neck and shorter ears, in addition to the shorter tail suggested by its name. Both species live in the Andes Mountains, especially the high snowy valleys from southern Peru and northern Bolivia to northern Chile and Argentina. The thick, dense fur of these rodents helps keep them warm in their cold, mountainous *habitat* (living area).

The short-tailed chinchilla (opposite page) and long-tailed chinchilla (above) are nearly identical, except for the lengths of the tails and size of their ears.

Diet. Chinchillas are social animals that live in large groups. During the day, they sleep in underground dens. At night, they come out to graze on grasses, roots, and other plant food.

Reproduction. Females give birth twice a year, usually to two or three young at a time. However, some females have as many as seven young at a time. The animals grow to adulthood in about a year. They may live for 10 years or more in the wild. The rapid reproduction rate of chinchillas is helping their populations recover from hundreds of years of capture and killing by people.

Threats. Hundreds of years ago, the Chincha and Inca Indians of South America ate chinchillas and used their fur to make clothing. Spanish explorers who arrived in South America in the 1500's named the rodents after the Chincha people. The Spanish immediately saw the value of the fur-bearing animals. Soon chinchilla fur was being sold in Europe. The popularity of the fur continued to grow in both Europe and North America. Chinchillas also grew in popularity as pets when people saw how clean, gentle, quiet, and easy to care for the rodents were.

Conservation. By the 1940's, the popularity of chinchillas had led to their near-extinction in the wild. That's when people in Europe and North and South America began breeding large numbers of chinchillas in captivity. As a result, captive-bred chinchillas met the demands of fur and pet lovers, while giving the wild chinchilla population a better chance of survival. This chance to survive increased when several South American nations passed laws to protect the wild populations.

Today, chinchillas remain rare in the wild. Some people continue to kill them, illegally. However, biologists hope that continued protection will allow the wild chinchilla populations to grow to healthy levels again.

Leontopithecus rosalia
Conservation status: Endangered

The golden lion tamarin is a small monkey with long, silky, shiny, golden-orange fur. The way that its fur surrounds its face makes the head of the monkey look almost like the head of a little lion surrounded by a thick mane.

The body of the golden lion tamarin can grow to a length of about 12 inches (30 centimeters), with the long tail adding another 16 inches (40 centimeters). The fully grown animal weighs no more than 1.8 pound (800 grams).

The monkeys have long, skinny fingers with sharp nails at the ends. They use their sharp nails to help them climb through trees and to pick or capture their favorite foods, which include insects, frogs, small birds, eggs, flowers, fruits, and even tree gum. These tamarins are *omnivores*—meaning that they eat just about anything they can fit into their mouths. Golden lion tamarins have unusual feet for a monkey. The big toe is on the back of the foot—similar to the big toe of a bird's foot.

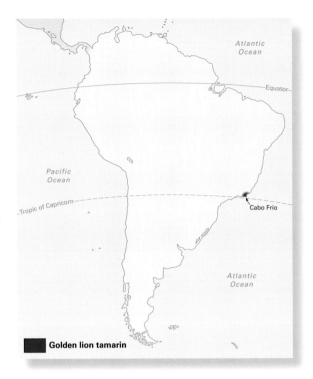

Golden lion tamarin

Habitat. The *arboreal* (tree-living) golden lion tamarin lives in the coastal tropical rain forests of southeastern Brazil. The monkeys usually stay in the trees about 5 to 20 feet (1.5 to 6 meters) above the ground. They get much of the water they need from plants called bromeliads. These plants grow attached to the trees, and they hold large amounts of water in their leaf clusters. The tamarins forage for food during the daytime. At night, they sleep in tree holes.

Reproduction. The tamarins move through the trees in small family groups called troops. Each troop is typically made up of a breeding male and female and one or two generations of offspring. Some groups also include additional family members. The monkeys communicate with a variety of high-pitched calls. The female most often gives birth to twins once a year—sometimes twice a year (if a lot of food is available that year). All members of the troop help care for the infants, carrying them around on their backs and grooming and feeding them.

Threats. The golden lion tamarin is endangered mainly because of the destruction of its rain forest *habitat* (living area). The human population along Brazil's Atlantic coast has expanded into rain forest areas—as have various *commercial* (business) operations. People have burned or cut down much of the forest to build cities, farms, roads, and industrial centers. Other parts of the forest have been felled to harvest timber. Only about 8 percent of the original rain forest remains in the region.

Conservation. By the early 1980's, fewer than 200 golden lion tamarins survived in *fragmented* (isolated) spots of rain forest habitat. Then, conservationists in Brazil and the United States began to work together to save this *species* (type) through a program involving captive breeding and habitat restoration. Many tamarins that have been born in zoos in the United States have been released into protected rain forest areas in Brazil. Thanks to these efforts, the species is finally on the road to recovery.

Captive breeding and habitat restoration programs are helping to increase the number of golden lion tamarins in their native rain forest habitat.

Cacajao calvus

Conservation status: Vulnerable

With a bald, bright red head on a body covered in a shaggy coat of long, reddish brown or orange-white fur, the bald uakari is impossible to mistake for any other monkey. Another unique feature is a very short tail, compared with the tails of most monkeys. Other monkeys use their long tails for balance as they move through trees. But the bald uakari seems to do fine with its stubby tail as it climbs through the trees of its rain forest *habitat* (living area) in the Amazon Basin. This *species* (type) is found in parts of Brazil and Peru, usually near rivers.

Appearance. Biologists believe that the uakari's bright red face serves as a sign that it is healthy. Uakaris that are sick with malaria—a common mosquito-born disease in the Amazon Basin—have pale faces. So a bright red face tells a potential mate that the individual is healthy and *immune* to (protected against) malaria. Those individuals are more attractive to potential mates and so more likely to be selected as breeding partners. Therefore, they are more likely to produce offspring that inherit the immunity. This is an example of how *natural selection* helps a species survive. According to this process, members of a species better suited to their environment leave more descendants than other members of the same species.

Diet. Bald uakaris range from 14 to 23 inches (36 to 58 centimeters) in length. The most they weigh is about 6.5 pounds (3 kilograms). They forage for plant food during the daytime. The favorite foods of the monkeys are fruits and nuts, but they also eat leaves, seeds, roots, and insects. They spend most of their time in the trees. They usually visit the ground only when food is hard to find in the trees, such as during droughts.

Uakaris spend the day alone, with their mates, or in small groups of no more than

Bald uakari

10 individuals. As night approaches, the monkeys gather together in larger groups to socialize, *groom* each other (remove ticks and other parasites from fur), rest, and sleep.

Reproduction. A large group of uakaris, called a troop, may have as many as 100 members. Females give birth to a single infant once every two years. This slow rate of reproduction means that the bald uakari population could not grow quickly even if the species were fully protected against threats.

Threats. But the bald uakari is not fully protected against threats. Some *indigenous* (native) people in the Amazon Basin kill the monkeys for food and capture them to use as bait for larger game. Some indigenous tribes, however, refuse to harm these monkeys because they think the uakaris look too much like little, red-faced people.

The rain forest habitat of the uakaris is shrinking as the trees are cut down, mainly by the timber industry. The downed forests are sometimes replaced with farmland.

The bald uakari's red face is a sign of good health, suggesting an individual that is immune from malaria. An uakari that is infected with the parasitic disease develops a pale face.

Ateles hybridus
Conservation status: Critically endangered

Spider monkeys are large monkeys with four long, skinny limbs and a long tail that they use as an extra limb. They can hang from tree branches and pick up objects with this *prehensile* (grasping) tail. The monkeys get their name from the way they sometimes hang upside down by grasping a branch with all four limbs and the tail. When they do that, they look like giant spiders to people on the ground. Several *species* (types) of spider monkey live in forests from central Mexico to central Bolivia. Many species are endangered, mainly because of the destruction of their *habitats* (living areas).

Habitat. The brown, or variegated, spider monkey is found in the southern regions of Central America and in the northern regions of South America. They can be identified by their *variegated* coloration—that ism, their color varies depending on the part of the body. Colors may also vary from one individual to another. The fur on the back, the upper parts of the limbs, and the head is light brown or dark reddish-brown. The fur on the stomach and lower parts of the limbs is whitish or buff-colored. The eyes, as in most mammals, are usually brown. But some individuals have blue eyes. Most of these monkeys live in the upper parts of old, tall trees in rain forests, where they forage for fruits, flowers, seeds, and other plant matter.

The body of the brown spider monkey is about 20 inches (50 centimeters) long, not counting the tail. The tail may be as long as 31 inches (80 centimeters). Like other spider monkeys, the brown spider monkey has the perfect body for living in trees and swinging from branch to branch. Its hands are shaped like hooks, with four long, curved fingers that firmly wrap around branches. The thumb is just a stub. The tip of the tail is naked, flexible, and grooved, helping it to get a good grip on branches. Few other monkeys are able to move so rapidly through treetops.

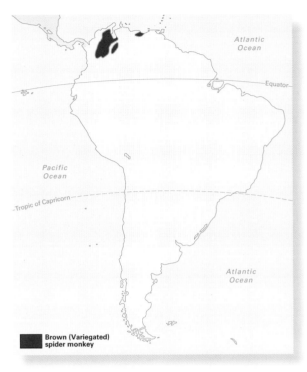

Brown (Variegated) spider monkey

Social life. Members of this species live in groups, or troops, that may have more than 20 members. A group usually breaks up to forage. It comes back together later. When members of the group get together again, the monkeys greet each other with loud calls, hug each other, wrap their tails together, and chase each other through the trees.

Young spider monkeys hang on to the mother's belly for the first few months of life. They then move to her back before later foraging on their own.

Threats. Biologists estimate that roughly 80 percent of the brown spider monkey population has been wiped out since about 1970. The main cause of this drastic population decline has been habitat destruction from agricultural development, logging, and human settlement.

The monkeys are also killed for meat and captured for sale as pets. The IUCN classifies this species as one of the 25 most endangered *primates* (the group of animals that includes monkeys, apes, and humans).

The brown spider monkey is among the most endangered members of the primate family. Its numbers have been greatly reduced by habitat loss.

Tremarctos ornatus

Conservation status: Vulnerable

A bear that wears glasses? That's what you might think from the "spectacled" part of the name of this bear *species* (type). The name comes from the whitish rings of fur that surround the eyes of some—but not all—of the bears. The rest of the bear's fur is usually brown or black with whitish-yellowish markings on the face, neck, and chest. Those markings vary from individual to individual. This animal is small for a bear, reaching a maximum length of about 6 feet (1.8 meters) and a maximum weight of about 340 pounds (154 kilograms). It is the only bear native to South America.

Habitat. The spectacled bear is also called the Andes bear, referring to the Andes Mountains of South America. It lives in the forests that grow on the slopes of these mountains. These forests, sometimes called "cloud forests," may be as high as 14,000 feet (4,300 meters). The bears often move to lower ground when they're looking for food. They forage mainly at night.

Diet. Fruits seem to be the spectacled bear's favorite food, but they also eat cactuses, palm leaves, and other plant matter. People have reported seeing the bears patiently sit in trees for several days as they wait for fruits to ripen. The bears have been known to strip bark to eat the soft wood beneath. They also eat insects, rodents, birds, and other small animals.

Reproduction. Spectacled bears spend most of their time alone—except during the breeding season. Females give birth to one to three cubs. The cubs are tiny and helpless when born. After about a month, they begin to walk around. But even after they can walk, they like to ride on the mother's back. The cubs may stay with her for as long as eight months. The male takes no part in raising the young. In fact, the mother has to protect her cubs against the father and other male bears because they try to eat the young.

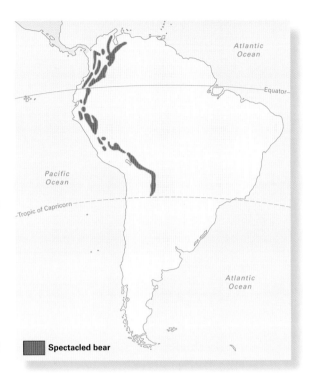

Spectacled bear

Threats. Fewer than 3,000 spectacled bears may exist today—though the remote *habitat* (living area) of the bears makes it difficult for scientists to obtain data about their population. What is known is that the spectacled bear's natural habitats have been broken up by cropland, ranches, roads, towns, and other human developments.

The conversion of natural forest and grassland to farmland and ranchland has put the bears into conflict with farmers and ranchers. These people kill the bears because the animals have been known to eat corn and small calves.

Other people hunt and kill the bears for their meat or their body parts. The body parts are sold to make traditional medicines. The bear cubs are also preyed on by pumas and jaguars.

Conservation. Spectacled bears are protected by laws that ban both their killing and the trade in their body parts. Much of their habitat is also legally protected. However, the governments in the Andes region have a hard time enforcing these laws.

The spectacled bear is the only bear native to South America. It is threatened by both habitat loss and hunting.

Leopardus jacobita

Conservation status: Endangered

The Andean cat, also known as the mountain or Andean mountain cat, is a medium-sized carnivore with beautiful, silvery gray fur that grows into a long, thick pelt. The coat is marked by yellowish-brown spots and stripes across the back and sides. The cat's long, fluffy tail measures as much as 19 inches (48 centimeters) in length—almost as long as the rest of the body, which ranges from 22 to 25 inches (57 to 64 centimeters) in length. The tail is marked by six to nine dark rings.

Habitat. These cats wrap their long, bushy tails around their bodies for warmth while they sleep in their high, cold *habitat* (living area) in the Andes Mountains. They can be found in some of the highest parts of these mountains in Argentina, Bolivia, Chile, and Peru, typically at elevations from 9,840 to 16,400 feet (3,000 to 5,000 meters). The ground there is rough, rocky, and dry, with the main plants being sparsely growing grasses and short shrubs. The cats' long tails and large feet help them keep their balance as they walk and run over the loose rocks and big boulders.

Threats. The preferred prey of Andean cats consists of viscachas, which are rodents that are related to chinchillas and resemble rabbits. Andean cats are not the only cats in the area that like to eat viscachas. A more *abundant* (great in number) species known as the pampas cat also preys on these rodents. Both species of cat also prey on chinchillas. Viscachas and chinchillas have declined in number because people hunt them for their fur and meat. The competition with pampas cats and the reduced number of viscachas and chinchillas are two reasons that the population of Andean cats has decreased.

Another reason for the endangered status of the Andean cat is hunting by *indigenous* (native) people known as the Aymara and Quechua. These people view the Andean cat as a special,

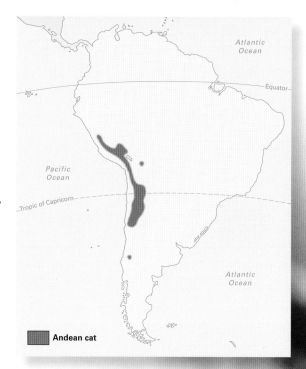

The Andean cat uses its long, bushy tail to cover itself when sleeping, keeping it warm in the cold, high elevations of the Andes Mountains.

sacred animal. They use the cat's dried, stuffed, decorated bodies in religious ceremonies. Other local people kill the cats for food, for their fur, or to make traditional medicines from the animals' body parts. Ranchers and farmers in the area sometimes kill Andean cats because they blame these meat-eaters for killing their livestock. Cattle grazing and mining activities have destroyed parts of the cats' habitat.

Conservation. Since the 1990's, scientists have studied the Andean cat population to better understand why it is declining and how it could be protected. More recently, they developed a conservation plan. The plan includes expanding the sizes of the protected areas in which the cats live, educating local people about the need to save the cats, and building up the populations of the cats' prey. Laws in Argentina, Bolivia, Chile, and Peru ban the hunting of Andean cats and the selling and owning of the cats or their body parts. However, government officials often have trouble enforcing these laws.

Glossary

Abundant Great in number.

Adaptation A trait of an organism that makes it better able to survive and reproduce in its environment.

Algae Seaweed.

Alien Nonnative.

Arboreal Living in or among trees.

Avian Having to do with birds.

Camouflage Coloration or other physical traits that protect an animal by making the animal hard to see.

Carapace Top shell.

Carrion Dead and decaying flesh.

Cartilage A tough, rubbery tissue that is more flexible than bone and not as hard.

Clearcutting Cutting down all the trees in an area.

Commercial Having to do with businesses and making money.

Continental shelf Part of a sea floor that slopes from the shore to about 330 feet (100 meters) deep.

Criteria Rules.

Crustaceans Animals with a hard shell, jointed body and appendages, and gills, that live mostly in water.

Deforestation The destruction or damaging of trees.

Dorsal fin Back fin.

El Niño and La Niña An interaction between Earth's atmosphere and the tropical waters of the Pacific Ocean that recurs every several years, resulting in changes in ocean currents and weather.

Elytra Hard coverings that protect the wings and body of certain insects.

Equator The imaginary circle around the middle of the planet that divides the Northern and Southern hemispheres.

Evolution by natural selection The theory that all species of living things developed gradually from a common ancestor over the course of many millions of years by a branching process.

Fossil fuel Coal, natural gas, and crude oil.

Fragmentation The breaking up of a habitat so that different parts are not connected.

Habitat The type of environment in which an organism lives.

Immunity Resistance.

Indigenous Native; refers to people whose ancestors were from the same region where the people are found today.

Invertebrates Animals without backbones.

Larvae Immature, wormlike forms.

Mariner A sailor.

Metamorphosis The process in which extreme changes in body form occur between the immature growing phase and the mature adult phase of certain animals.

Mutualism Any relationship between two different species in which both species benefit.

Natural selection Refers to the main way in which scientists believe the evolution of species works—by a process in which members of a species better suited to their environment leave more descendants than other members of the same species.

Omnivore An animal that eats a wide variety of both animal and plant food.

Overexploited A species of animal that is fished or hunted to the point that its population becomes greatly reduced and threatened.

Poaching Illegal hunting or killing of animals.

Prehensile Capable of grasping or holding on.

Primate The group of animals that includes monkeys, apes, and human beings.

Proboscis Snout.

Pupa Stage of an insect metamorphosis between the larval and the winged adult stages.

Range The area in which a species naturally occurs.

Salinity Level of salt in water.

Sand bar A ridge of sand formed by the action of ocean tides or river currents.

Sediment Soil and other matter carried by water.

Species A group of animals that have certain permanent characteristics in common and are able to interbreed.

Toxic Poisonous.

Tympanum In frogs, the round outer membrane that sends sound waves to the inner ear.

Variegated Varied in appearance, usually a pattern of alternating light and dark colors.

Books

Hammond, Paula. *The Atlas of Endangered Animals: Wildlife Under Threat Around the World.* Tarrytown, NY: Marshall Cavendish, 2010. Print.

Hoare, Ben, and Tom Jackson. *Endangered Animals.* New York: DK Pub., 2010. Print.

Silhol, Sandrine, Gaëlle Guérive, and Marie Doucedame. *Extraordinary Endangered Animals. New York: Abrams Books for Young Readers,* 2011. Print.

Wild Animal Atlas: Earth's Astonishing Animals and Where They Live. Washington, DC: National Geographic, 2010. Print.

Websites

Arkive. Wildscreen, 2014. Web. 14 May 2014.

"Endangered Animals of the Americas." *National Geographic Education.* National Geographic Society, 2014. Web. 14 May 2014.

"Especies Fact Sheets." *Kids' Planet.* Defenders of Wildlife, n.d. Web. 14 May 2014.

"The Galápagos." *World Wildlife Fund.* World Wildlife Fund, 2014. Web. 14 May 2014.

Tregaskis, Shiona. "The world's extinct and endangered species – interactive map." *The Guardian.* Guardian News and Media Limited, 3 Sept. 2012. Web. 14 May 2014.

Organizations *for helping endangered animals*

Alaska Wildlife Adoption
By adopting an animal at the Alaska Wildlife Conservation Center, you can enjoy animal parenthood without all the work.
http://www.alaskawildlife.org/support /alaska-wildlife-adoption/

Defenders of Wildlife
Founded in 1947, Defenders of Wildlife is a major national conservation organization focused on wildlife and habitat conservation.
http://www.defenders.org/take-action

National Geographic – Big Cats Initiative
National Geographic, along with Dereck and Beverly Joubert, launched the Big Cats Initiative to raise awareness and implement change to the dire situation facing big cats.
http://animals.nationalgeographic.com/animals /big-cats-initiative/

National Geographic – The Ocean Initiative
National Geographic's Ocean Initiative helps identify and support individuals and organizations that are using creative and entrepreneurial approaches to marine conservation.
http://ocean.nationalgeographic.com/ocean /about-ocean-initiative/

National Wildlife Federation – Adoption Center
Symbolically adopt your favorite species and at the same time support the National Wildlife Federation's important work protecting wildlife and connecting people to nature.
http://www.shopnwf.org/Adoption-Center/index.cat

Neighbor Ape
Neighbor Ape strives to conserve the habitat of wild chimpanzees in southeastern Senegal, to protect the chimpanzees themselves, and to provide for the well-being of the Senegalese people who have traditionally lived in the area alongside these chimpanzees.
http://www.globalgiving.org/donate/10235 /neighbor-ape/

Smithsonian National Zoo – Adopt a Species
The Adopt a Species program supports the National Zoo's extraordinary work in the conservation and care of the world's rarest animals.
http://nationalzoo.si.edu/support/adoptspecies/

World Wildlife Fund
World Wildlife Fund works in 100 countries and is supported by over 1 million members in the United States and close to 5 million globally.
http://www.worldwildlife.org/how-to-help

Index

Acknowledgments

The publishers acknowledge the following sources for illustrations. Credits read from top to bottom, left to right, on their respective pages. All maps, charts, and diagrams were prepared by the staff unless otherwise noted.

COVER © Craig Lovell, Eagle Visions Photography/ Alamy Images; © vdbvsl/Alamy Images
4 © vdbvsl/Alamy Images
7 Gregory G. Dimijian, Science Source
9 © Carlos Bustamante; © Shutterstock
11 © Jesse Cancelmo, Alamy Images
13 © David & Micha Sheldon, Alamy Images
15 © Thomas Marent, Visuals Unlimited
17 © Minden Pictures/SuperStock
19 © Ritterbach, Alamy Images
21 © imageBROKER/Alamy Images
23 © Robert Bannister, Alamy Images
25 © David Sewell, Alamy Images
27 © Henk Meijer, Alamy Images
28 © Konrad Wothe, Nature Picture Library
29 © Juniors Bildarchiv/Alamy Images
31 © Dave G. Houser, Alamy Images
33 © Paul Crum, Science Source
34 © Michael DeFreitas, Alamy Images
35 © Luciano Candisani, Minden Pictures
37 © Robert Pickett, Alamy Images
39 © Thomas Marent, Rolfnp/Alamy Images
41 © imageBROKER/Alamy Images
43 © Pete Oxford, Nature Picture Library
45 © Gunter Ziesler, Getty Images